BAKUMAN。

STORY BY TSUGUMI OHBA
ART BY TAKESHI OBATA

From the creators of *Death Note*

The mystery behind manga making REVEALED!

Average student Moritaka Mashiro enjoys drawing for fun. When his classmate and aspiring writer Akito Takagi discovers his talent, he begs to team up. But what exactly does it take to make it in the manga-publishing world?

Bakuman。, Vol. 1
ISBN: 978-1-4215-3513-5
$9.99 US / $12.99 CAN *

Manga on sale at **store.viz.com**
Also available at your local bookstore or comic store

www.shonenjump.com

RATED T FOR TEEN
ratings.viz.com

VIZ media
www.viz.com

IN THE NEXT VOLUME...

MELZEZ DOOR

Ageha's fully aware of how little he understands his newfound abilities. But when a mysterious millionaire introduces him to a group of Psionist kids who also have powers, his training ramps up and his confidence grows. Has he learned enough to survive the game of Psyren? A glimpse into the dark future of our world has him not so sure.

Available MAY 2012!

Afterword

AND SO, VOLUME 3
HAS NOW MADE
IT TO THE SHELVES!
(APPLAUSE!)

EVERY DAY IS FULL OF DRAFTING.
I DRAW STORYBOARDS, I
STRUGGLE, I DRAW DRAFTS...
I DRAW, I THINK, I STRUGGLE
AND DRAW...LOOKING BACK,
IT'S ALWAYS THE SAME.
DURING EVERY MOMENT THAT
I'M WORKING, I THINK UP
STORYBOARDS, AND I DRAW
SCENES I'VE NEVER DRAWN
BEFORE...SO STRANGELY ENOUGH,
IT STILL ALWAYS FEELS FRESH.
AS I WORK WITH MY STAFF,
I'M REALIZING THAT THAT'S HOW
IT IS. ANYWAY, SEE YOU AGAIN
IN VOLUME 4! (SORRY
TO RAMBLE...)

I DON'T WANT TO DIE IN FRONT OF AGEHA– HE'S THE ONE WHO WOUNDED ME.
HE SAVED ME– I DON'T WANT HIM TO FEEL THAT HE TOOK MY LIFE.
I'M STAYING BEHIND ON MY OWN.
I DON'T INTEND TO GO QUIETLY TO MY GRAVE. PERHAPS SOMEWHERE IN THIS WORLD I CAN FIND A WAY TO SURVIVE IN THIS TABOO BODY.
EVEN WITH NO CARD, I'LL FIND A WAY.
I WANTED TO COME TO THIS WORLD.
WAIT FOR ME, ASAGA.
I PROMISE TO FIND YOU AGAIN.
ON THESE TWO FEET...
VOL. 3 DRAGON / END

HE LEFT.
HE SAID HE'D LOST HIS CARD AND HE WAS GOING TO LOOK FOR IT.
HE WAS GOING TO LOOK FOR IT?!
WHY DIDN'T HE TELL US?!
YOU WERE ALL DESPERATE WITH WORRY OVER SAVING ASAGA. I THINK HE DIDN'T WANT TO CAUSE YOU ANY MORE TROUBLE.
HE SAID HE WAS SORRY, AND THAT HE UNDER-STANDS IF YOU'RE MAD.
BUT THAT'S CRAZY! WHAT'LL WE TELL HIRYU?!
HOW COULD HE?
...
I KNOW MY DEATH IS NEAR.
WHEN THIS ORB LOSES ITS STRENGTH, I'LL DIE WITH IT.

HE DIDN'T HAVE A CARD!!
TATSUO DIDN'T HAVE A CARD!!
?!
BUT WHY DID HE LIE?!
SO... HE CAN'T COME BACK?
HE KNEW HE COULDN'T COME HOME.
HE JUST DIDN'T SAY ANYTHING SO WE WOULDN'T NOTICE.
PLES
VWHOOM
!!
WHERE ARE WE?! WE'RE BACK, AREN'T WE?
OBORO! WHERE'S TATSUO ?!
SHWA

LES ONE
デジタル110番
ONE
...
TATSUO!!
WHY?! IDIOT!!

POINTS REMAINING
48
POINTS REMAINING
45
...
...
THANK YOU.
GOOD-BYE.
TATSUO ?!
DO YOU REALLY HAVE YOUR CA-
VWAHHHH

WHAT?
THAT HOUSE OVER THERE...
OH!!
OBORO. WILL YOU HOLD THIS WHILE I GET THE RECEIVER?
SURE.
VWOON
YOU GO NEXT, AGEHA.
OKAY.
BWOOSH

THE PENDANT I GAVE ASAGA...
...AND THE ONE I KEPT LOCKED AWAY IN MY DESK!
THANK YOU...
THANK YOU FOR COMING AFTER ME, ASAGA!
TA-TSUO?
I'LL GO LAST. HURRY UP AND TAKE ASAGA BACK!
...
HMM?
FWHOOO

ALRIGHT, EVERYONE. FOLLOW ME.
POINTS REMAINING
30
POINTS REMAINING
27
FWOOSH
SHE'S GONE ?!
ALRIGHT, NEXT!
ASAGA, I'M SO SORRY. I'M SO SORRY I DID THIS TO YOU...

HOME ...
DON'T WORRY. WHEN WE GET HOME, I'M SURE SOMEBODY CAN HELP YOU. THERE HAS TO BE A WAY!
THAT'S ALRIGHT. I GUESS I ALREADY KNEW THAT, SOMEHOW.
IT'S PART OF ME, NOW.
I...
GET YOUR CARDS OUT, EVERY-ONE.
LET'S GO.
I HAVE MY CARD.
OH... TA-TSUO?
OH, OKAY.
YOU GO FIRST, AMA-MIYA.
OKAY.
BWHOOM

IS IT THIS WAY?
IT'S RIGHT OVER THERE, SEE? YOUR SENSE OF DIRECTION BLOWS!
VWHOOO
I CAN'T BELIEVE THIS IS JAPAN'S FUTURE.
WE'RE IN TOYO-GUCHI CITY.
NO WAY!
THIS IS BAD.
IT'S COM-PLETELY EMBEDDED IN YOUR SYSTEM.
I'M SORRY, BUT I'M AFRAID I'M POWER-LESS TO REMOVE IT.

VWAAA
SHOOM
THAT'S THE BEST I CAN DO. THE WOUND'S CLOSED, AT LEAST.
THIS IS BAD. HE'S STILL UNCONSCIOUS.
TUNK
AMAMIYA? HIRYU'S...
WE SHOULD HURRY UP AND GET HIM BACK TO OUR TIME. LET'S HEAD FOR THE GATE!
GOOD IDEA!
HYUP

WAAAH
HUH?
WAAAAAAAH
DON'T FORGET ABOUT ME, GUYS!!
TAKE ME WITH YOU, YOU HEARTLESS TRAITORS!!
OH, RIGHT. HIM.
I'LL GO GET HIM. I NEED TO GET MY STUFF ANYWAY.
IF THE WORM ATTACKS YOU, I'LL BLOW MY WHISTLE AGAIN.
WHOOOO
A PIGGY-BACK RIDE FROM A GIRL? IT'S LIKE A DREAM COME TRUE!
HOW BOUT YOU TAKE CARE OF ME LIKE THIS FOR THE REST OF OUR LIVES?
DON'T MAKE ME DROP YOU...

THE LEADER...
...OF THE TABOO?
I'VE BEEN HERE—OR RATHER, MY BODY HAS—EVER SINCE.
WHENEVER MY MIND SURFACED FOR A MOMENT...
...I WAS BOTH RELIEVED AND ANGUISHED TO DISCOVER I WAS STILL ALIVE.
THANK YOU... IT WAS YOUR POWERS THAT SAVED ME.
!
IT WAS...
...TOTAL CHANCE. I WAS JUST LUCKY.
I THOUGHT FATE WAS ON YOUR SIDE, AGEHA!
GOOD POINT.
OKAY, I'LL TAKE CREDIT.

IF YOU DISCOVER ANY INTRUDERS...
...ANNIHILATE THEM!!
LUB-
DUB
KILL ANY PSIONISTS WHO RESIST US!
YOU'RE NOW A POWERFUL PSIONIST YOURSELF!
KILL!

WORTH-LESS SIMPLE-TONS!
VWHOOO
I'LL NEVER GET ANY INFORMATION OUT OF HIM NOW!
VERY WELL. I'LL PUT YOU TO USE PATROLLING AN AREA WHERE WE NEED MORE SURVEILLANCE.
I HOPE YOU'LL PROVE YOURSELF A BIT MORE USEFUL THAN THESE BRAINLESS BLOBS...

THAT BLOND MAN WITH HIS STRANGE DRESS AND MONSTROUS ATTENDANTS...
BUT HE, TOO, HAD A GLOWING BLOB ON HIS CHEST.
BY THE WAY, BOY... WHAT WERE YOU DOING IN THIS AREA?
WHERE DID YOU COME FROM?
HA!
IDIOTS! HE'S ALREADY LOST HIMSELF!! HE'S NO GOOD ANYMORE!
WHY DID YOU OPERATE BEFORE I GOT HERE?
?!
...HAD A COM-PLETELY HUMAN FORM.

I FELT LIKE I WAS LOSING TRACK OF WHO I WAS...
KOFF KOFF
HIM?
HE'S JUST A CHILD!
I SUPPOSE I SHOULD CON-GRATULATE YOU.
YOU'VE MANAGED TO RETAIN YOUR HUMAN FORM ADMIRABLY.

DON'T WORRY ABOUT THAT. I'M MAKING HIM BETTER.
NOW, WOULD YOU MIND GIVING US SOME SPACE?
...
TATSUO, DO YOU REMEMBER WHAT HAPPENED TO YOU AFTER THEY SEALED AWAY YOUR IDENTITY?
FRAG-MENTS OF IT. IT WAS AS IF MY CONSCIOUS MIND CAME AND WENT.
THE TABOO CAPTURED YOU AND IMPLANTED A NUCLEUS IN YOUR BODY!
WILL YOU TELL US WHAT HAPPENED AFTER THAT?
...
I GUESS IT WAS NOT LONG AFTER THEY IMPLANTED MY NUCLEUS ...

THIS NUCLEUS SEALED AWAY MY IDENTITY.
THANKS TO YOU, MY CONSCIOUSNESS WAS FINALLY ABLE TO RESURFACE.
CALL.25: I'LL FIND A WAY HOME
YOU'RE REALLY SANE AGAIN NOW?
YOU'RE NOT GOING TO GO BERSERK ON US AGAIN, ARE YOU?
I THINK I'M OKAY NOW.
I CAN TELL... THIS IS PART OF MY BODY NOW.
I CAN REMEMBER WHAT'S BEEN HAPPENING.
I WAS WATCHING EVERYTHING. BUT I FELT LIKE I WAS IN SOMEONE ELSE'S BODY.
THE MEMORY OF WHAT I DID TO ASAGA...
...IS BURNED INTO MY BRAIN!

ASAGA'S HAIR IS BROWN.

IS THAT SO?

THE WAY THE SUN SHINES ON IT MAKES IT HARD TO TELL.

IT'S BROWN, HUH?

TATSUO !!
YOU DID IT.
MY POWERS ARE GONE.
BUT NOW THANKS TO YOU, I REMEMBER WHO I AM.
WHEEZ
...
SHF
SHF
SHP
ASAGA ...

FWEE
TEEE
SHLO
KRHEE!
IT TAKES PRAC-TICE.
Y-YOU ...

IT WON'T WHISTLE!
AM I USING IT WRONG?
YOSHINA! YOU TRY!
!!
A-ARE YOU SURE, AMAMIYA?
WHAT'S THE PROBLEM, YOSHINA? HURRY UP AND DO IT!
GIVE IT TO ME.
YOU !!

SHOOP
SHLOOK
ATTA GIRL, AMA-MIYA!
FWOO
HUH?
...

BAM
BAM
BE STILL.
IT STILL DOESN'T KNOW EXACTLY WHERE WE ARE.
DON'T MAKE ANY LOUD SOUNDS.
OBORO, CONTINUE YOUR CURE...
LUB-DUB
LUB-DUB
THE MASK!

HUH?
IS HE ALL BETTER?
NOPE, NOT YET.
BUT I'M GETTING BORED OF THIS.
DON'T STOP!!
DON'T STOP, YOU MORON!!
WELL, I SHOULD HAVE THE RIGHT TO CHOOSE! WHO I WANT TO HOLD CLOSE AND WHEN I WANT TO HOLD THEM!
SHUT UP! DON'T BE RIDICULOUS!
WITH YOU, I FELT LIKE HOLDING YOU CLOSE, SO I DIDN'T GET BORED.
QUIT CREEPING ME OUT AND FINISH HEALING HIM ALREADY!!
RUMBLE RUMBLE RUMBLE
IF WE WASTE TIME, THAT GIANT WORM MIGHT COME BACK!!

I GOT THE MASK.
LET'S FIND KIRISAKI AND HEAD FOR THE GATE.
WE WON'T BE ABLE TO GO ANYWHERE TILL ASAGA'S HEALED.
I WONDER IF I...
...KILLED TATSUO?
...
YOU AND ASAGA DID EVERY-THING YOU COULD.
THIS WORLD-PSYREN-IS WHAT KILLED TATSUO.
HEY, AGEHA...
...CAN I STOP HEALING HIM NOW?

C'MON!
PAT
!
DON'T CRY!
WE MADE IT, DIDN'T WE?
I NEVER BREAK MY PROMISES!
YEAH, BUT...
...YOU ALMOST DID!
DON'T BE DUMB!
DON'T YOU KNOW FATE'S ON MY SIDE?
I DON'T LIKE ARGUING WITH YOSHINA.
HE'S TOO THICK-WITTED TO EVER UNDERSTAND...
...OTHER PEOPLE'S FEELINGS, AND STUFF LIKE THAT...

CURE IS THE ABILITY TO APPLY ONE'S OWN ENHANCE POWERS TO SOMEONE ELSE.
YOU USE ENHANCE TO ENHANCE YOUR HEALING ABILITIES AND BLAST TO CONVEY IT TO ANOTHER PERSON'S BODY... IT'S CALLED CURE, AND IT'S A SPECIAL TYPE OF PSI ONLY CERTAIN PSIONISTS CAN WIELD...
CHAK
BOO-HOO-HOO
HUH!?
OH, THANK YOU!
I'M SO GLAD!
I TOLD YOU TWO NOT TO GET YOURSELVES KILLED!!
AND BOTH OF YOU... BOTH OF YOU NEARLY BROKE YOUR PROMISE!!

OOF
KRAK
WH-WHAT'S HE DOING?
UNH
I'M TELLING YOU, IT'S OKAY!
!!
THE WOUND'S DEEP, BUT IT MISSED HIS ORGANS.
IT'S ALL RIGHT. IT'LL TAKE SOME TIME, BUT HE'LL BE OKAY.
HE'S USING CURE?
HE'S A CURE PSIONIST ?!
CURE ?

VWHOO...
HEAL HIM?
YOU MEAN... HE CAN HEAL ASAGA?
YES. JUST LEAVE IT TO MOCHI-ZUKI.
WHAT?! I DON'T BELIEVE IT!!
IT'S OBORO.
YOU CAN CALL ME OBORO, AGEHA.
ALL RIGHT ...

I'VE EXPERIENCED THE SAME POWER BEFORE, WITH MY OWN PERSON.
THAT'S WHY I WAS ABLE TO SAVE YOU.
I'LL HAVE TO THANK THAT BOY AGAIN WHEN I GET A CHANCE.
HE'S BETTER.
WHAT ?!
YOU USED ME AS A GUINEA PIG FOR YOUR FIRST PSI EXPERIMENT ?!
GASP
HIRYU !!
HIRYU ...
OH, ASAGA ?
HIRYU'S DYING! YOU HAVE TO SAVE HIM TOO, OBORO!!
WE'VE GOT TO FIND THEM! THEY CAN'T BE FAR FROM HERE!!
VWHOOO

VWHOOOO
...!!
?! HRG... WAS I... ASLEEP?
MY HEAD SUDDENLY FEELS SO MUCH LIGHTER ...
YOU WERE DYING OF BRAIN DAMAGE.
OH, YOSHINA! I'M SO GLAD YOU'RE ALL RIGHT!
OOF
AAAUGH !!
WH- WHAT DID YOU DO TO ME?!
WAS THAT... YOUR PSI?!
I CURED YOU. I WANTED TO CURE YOU, SO I DID.

MY INTUITION TELLS ME YOU'RE AN IMPORTANT PIECE IN THE PUZZLE THAT IS MY LIFE!
VWHOOO
WHY, I'M MOVED TO TEARS BY THE THOUGHT OF YOUR DEATH!
I WANT YOU TO LIVE... FOR ME!

MY LIFE'S JUST STARTING TO GET INTEREST-ING!
I CAN'T HAVE ANY ESSENTIAL PIECES MISSING!
IF YOU DIE ...
... WHERE'S THE FUN IN THAT?

NO!!
DON'T TELL ME HE'S...
... DYING ?!
YOU'RE NOT... GOING TO DIE, ARE YOU ?!
NO!! NO WAY!! WAKE UP!!
WE'VE ONLY JUST MET!
WHY DO YOU HAVE TO DIE NOW?!
YOU CAN'T !!
I WON'T LET YOU!!

OH, WELL! I'LL GET IN ON THE ACTION NEXT TIME!
NEXT TIME, I'M SURE I'LL GET THE CHANCE...
...TO WIELD THIS MYSTERIOUS POWER I FEEL WELLING UP WITHIN ME!!
PSI, IS IT?
HOW THRILLING!!
I HOPE IT'S A DESTRUCTIVE POWER!!
MORE POWERFUL EVEN THAN YOURS, I HOPE! I'LL LEARN TO WIELD PSI WITH TREMENDOUSLY DESTRUCTIVE POWER!! HEE-HEE!!
HEY, WHAT'S WRONG?
FWUMP
?! YOSHINA?!

I SHOULD'VE COME SOONER.
WELL, WELL!
AREN'T YOU FULL OF SURPRISES !!
THAT POWER OF YOURS IS THE VERY INCARNATION OF DE-STRUCTION!
TOO BAD I ONLY GOT TO OBSERVE FROM AFAR...
SHP
...
LOOKS LIKE THERE'S NOTHING LEFT FOR ME TO DO.

...
WHAT ...
...HAVE I DONE?
CALL.24: REVIVAL
TATSUO ...?
I'M...
...SO... SLEEPY...
SHP

WHEEZ
WHUMP
...!!
GHASA
GHASA
VWHOOO
KA-THUMP

KR AKK
IT'S GONE!
FWUMP
FWHOO
WOBBLE
YOSHINA ...?! YOSHINA !!

SHWIT
HAHH... HAHH... THAT WAS A CLOSE ONE...
IF I HADN'T STOPPED USING ENHANCE, IT WOULD'VE SKEWERED ME!!

VWAOW
YEEP!
KHHHR
KHHHR
!!
BOOSH

WHAT!?
NGHA!!
ARGH!
IT'S SWELLING FROM ABSORBING ALL THAT BLAST ENERGY!
!!
OH NO! IF IT REACTS TO PSIONIC ENERGY...
MAYBE IT'S DRAWN TO ENHANCERS TOO!
KRRAKK

!!
DOES THE ENERGY ITSELF HAVE ITS OWN WILL? IF YOSHINA ISN'T EVEN ABLE TO CONTROL IT, WHY DID IT PROTECT ME?
BLRB
BLBUBABRLK
DON'T TELL ME IT RESPONDS TO PSIONIC ENERGY...?!

LOOK AT IT GO!!
IF WE HADN'T GOTTEN OUT OF THERE, WE'D HAVE BEEN TOTALLY ANNIHILATED!
IT'S LIKE A VORTEX...
...THAT OBLITERATES EVERYTHING IT TOUCHES!!

!!
VWHRrr
THAT WAS CLOSE !!
VHHRRr

KCHUNG
WAVER
!!
KA
BOOM
GO, AMA-
MIYA
!!
VWOOM

HAHH
HAHH
!!
THAT BLACK SPHERE...
...IS THE FORM YOSHINA'S PSI TAKES!
IT ERASES ANYTHING IN ITS PATH!
AMAMIYA! YOU NEED TO GET OUT OF HERE!
GET AWAY FROM ME! NOW!
I CAN'T CONTROL IT! IT'S GETTING STRONGER AND STRONGER!!
IT HAS A WILL OF ITS OWN...
IF YOU DON'T GET OUT OF HERE, YOU'LL BE KILLED!
?!

HGH ...
HAHH
VWHHOO
SHWAAH
IN-CRED-IBLE!!
IT ABSORBED THE BLAST!!
YOSHINA'S PSI SWALLOWED IT UP!!

KSHMMASH
ZHWAAHH
?!
YOSHINA ?!

W-
WHAT
?!
BWA-
HA-HA-
HA-HA
!!
AMAMIYA
!!
HE'S
AIMING
YOUR
WAY!!
BOOM
!!

BUT YOU...
HURRY UP AND GO!!
LOOK!!
HE JUST FINISHED RELOADING!!
BREEEEM
HE WAS SAVING IT UP! THAT SON-OF-A...
EVEN IF HE WAS TIRED, HE WAS TAKING WAY TOO LONG THE SECOND TIME!!
HE FAKED US OUT!! HE WANTED TO KNOW WHAT WE WERE PLOTTING-HE WANTED US TO MAKE OUR MOVE!!

AUGH!!
AAAUGH!!
WAAAH!
ASAGA... ASAGA...
YOU TAKE CARE OF HIRYU. HE'S STILL ALIVE, RIGHT?
I'LL HANDLE... THE REST...

SHP
BACKING OFF? SO YOU'RE CAPABLE OF FEAR, EH?
SHP
THEN WHY...
HOW COULD YOU...
TUNK
VWHSHH
SHOONK
SHOONK
SHLOO
...
!!
VWHSH
NO!!
YOSHINA !!
DON'T!! YOU'LL CRUSH YOUR BRAIN!!
THAT DOESN'T MATTER !!

RR
RMBLE
KRRKKLE
SHOOM

THE WORM IS HOLDING BACK...
IT'S SCARED!!
YOSHINA'S BLOW REALLY SCARED IT!
NOW'S MY CHANCE!!
I'VE GOT A TERRIBLE FEELING ABOUT THIS.
PLEASE... PLEASE, BOTH BE OKAY WHEN I FIND YOU...

ZHHR-HB
CALL.23: DESTRUCTION
INTENSE PSIONIC WAVES...
VWHOO
DON'T TELL ME... IT'S ACTUALLY YOSHINA?!
GHRHAOW
!

MOVE.
GET IN MY WAY AND I'LL KILL YOU.

GET AWAY FROM HIRYU.

!!
THIS ENERGY ...?! YOSHINA ...?!
KA-KA-KA-
BOOOM

ZHHRMM
AAAUGH!!
IS THAT ...
... YOUR ANSWER ?!
?!

WA-
HA-
HA
HA-
HA-
HA-
HA
!!

HIRYUUUU!!

KSHH
OW-
LET'S GO HOME ...
... TATSUO ...

THE TWO OF US TOGETHER ARE ONE DRAGON!
ONE DRAGON, TOGETHER!
ONE DRAGON, TO-GETHER!
I STILL WEAR IT...
KA-THUMP

TATSUO! HANG IN THERE!
WHERE... HIRYU... WHO AM I?! WHAT ON EARTH ...?!
AUGH... HRAU-GGHH!
SOME-THING'S WRONG !!
GET BACK, HIRYU !!
I'M HERE !!
DON'T WORRY !!
CHAK
I'LL STAY WITH YOU!!
KEEP FIGHTING, TATSUO !!
IT'S ALL RIGHT-YOU'LL FIND YOUR WAY BACK!
THEY HAVEN'T BROKEN YOU!!
YOU WANTED TO BE A HERO, REMEM-BER?
I'M THE BODY, AND YOU'RE THE BRAINS, REMEMBER? TATSUO!!
YOU'VE GOT TO RECOVER YOUR TRUE SELF!!

HIRYU... HOW WAS... HOW WAS THE... GAME?
?!
DID YOU HIT... ANOTHER GRAND SLAM?
HA HA! WHAT'RE YOU TALKING ABOUT!?
YOU PROMISED ME WE'D GO RIDE BIKES TOGETHER WHEN I LEARNED HOW, RIGHT?
DON'T FORGET!
UH-OH.
HIS MEMORY'S A COMPLETE JUMBLE...
AH... AAAUGH !!
TATSUO ?!
KA-THUMP
KA-THUMP
I CAN'T REMEMBER ANYTHING!! AUGGH!!
WHO ON EARTH AM I?!

BLINK
!!
YOU'RE AWAKE ...
... TATSUO.
HIRYU?
!!
TATSUO? TATSUO!! YOU REMEMBER ME!!

VWHOOO
THE ROUND THING ON TATSUO'S CHEST ISN'T GLOWING AS BRIGHTLY ANYMORE.
DOES THAT MEAN HIS TABOO POWER IS WANING?
WAIT A SEC— THIS IS OUR CHANCE!
ARGH ...
WOBBLE
MAN, THAT WAS A SERIOUS PUNCH ...
GOTTA DESTROY THAT GUN!

GRRR
NGH ...
SLUMP
KA-BASH
HIRYU !!
GAK
HAHH
TA-TSUO ...

I CAME TO FIND YOU!!
I'M HERE TO BRING YOU HOME!
!!
LOOK INTO MY EYES!!
COME ON, TATSUO-WAKE UP!!
HIRYU...
ZAP
ZZZ
ZZZT

EVEN IF MY BRAIN'S ABOUT TO EXPLODE...
...I WON'T LET YOU GO!
URK
VWWSH
KSHHHH
I WON'T ACCEPT YOU FORGETTING ABOUT ME, TATSUO!!
HIRYU ASAGA, YOUR CHILDHOOD FRIEND!
IT'S HIRYU!
VA-THUMP

HRG!
YIKES! HE GOT FREE!
VHRR
!?

VWWSH
CALL.22: DRAGON
WATCH OUT, HIRYU!
SIZZLE SIZZLE
KH
HR
AH

FUBUKI (24), THE OLDER SISTER WHO GETS
SUDDENLY AFFECTIONATE ONCE A YEAR.

Hey, Aggy! Wanna hang out today?
AUGH!

DRAGON TAIL!
GRRRRR
SEE, TATSUO? IT'S NOTHING TO BRAG ABOUT YET, BUT...
...THIS IS WHAT I CAN DO.
HIRYU !!

BOOM
!!
KHHK
VWHOO
?!
I'M OVER HERE.

SHOOM

VWHOOO
THEY SAY A HERO DESCENDS FROM ABOVE AT THE LAST MINUTE!
ZING

IF HE USES UP HIS PSI AND CAN NO LONGER WIELD STRENGTH...
...YOU HAVE A CHANCE OF STOPPING HIM.
PAM
NNAG
OH NO...
CONCEN-TRATE ON EVASIVE STRATE-GIES.
NORMAL ATTACKS WILL BE PRACTICALLY USELESS AGAINST HIS FORTIFIED BODY!
AND IF HE EVER GETS HOLD OF YOU...

EARLIER THAT DAY...
LISTEN, YOU TWO. WHEN YOU FACE OFF WITH HIM, WATCH OUT FOR HIS ENHANCE.
ACTUALLY, ENHANCE COMES IN DIFFERENT TYPES.
TYPES?
BASICALLY, THERE'S TWO MAIN CATEGORIES: SENSE, WHICH RELATES TO SENSORY PERCEPTIONS...
...AND STRENGTH, WHICH RELATES TO MUSCULAR AND PHYSICAL ABILITIES.
Enhance
Strength
Sense
SENSE AND STRENGTH, HUH?
YES. I THINK TATSUO ONLY USES THE LATTER.
THERE'S NOTHING SPECIAL ABOUT HIS COORDINATION, REFLEXES AND SENSORY PERCEPTIONS.
THAT MEANS YOU GUYS STAND A CHANCE.
JUST LIKE THAT MONSTER DUDE YOU FOUGHT BEFORE?
RIGHT.
ALSO, HE'S DEPLETED FROM FIRING MULTIPLE SHOTS OF BLAST ENERGY, AND HE'S COMPENSATING FOR HIS ORIGINAL PHYSICAL DISABILITIES.
IT'S EXHAUSTING USING TWO TYPES OF PSI AT ONCE.
THERE'S A LIMIT TO OUR PSIONIC ENERGIES.
THE FACT THAT IT'S TAKING HIM LONGER TO RELOAD THE SECOND TIME IS PROOF OF THAT.
HE'S GOT TO BE PRETTY WORN OUT BY NOW.

FWAM
HEY, YOU CAN DO BETTER THAN THAT.
WHY DONCHA PUT DOWN YOUR GUN?
YOU'RE BOTH FASTER AND STRONGER THAN ME.
BUT YOU'RE BEING WAY TOO SLOPPY.
WA-
PAH
SHOOP
I CAN TELL YOU'RE NOT USED TO FIGHTING.
YOU'VE GOTTA MAKE YOUR MOVEMENTS MORE COMPACT.

ZOOM
NOW THAT'S FAST.
ENHANCE...
VWASHH

THAT WAS WHY...
MONEY?
WHAT MONEY?
...I RESOLVED TO CHANGE.
YOU KNOW WHAT I'M TALKING ABOUT. THE MONEY YOU TOOK FROM THE GUYS IN MY CLASS YESTERDAY.
COUGH IT UP. ALL OF IT.
YOU'VE GOT SOME NERVE, KID.
WHAT'S YOUR NAME?
I DECIDED TO BECOME A HERO...
...SO THAT I COULD FACE YOU PROUDLY WHEN OUR PATHS CROSSED AGAIN.
DRAGON.

IT WAS A HAND-CARVED WOODEN PENDANT.
THE MIRACLE DRAGON—TATSUO AS THE HEAD, ME AS THE BODY.
TATSUO'S TRUE FEELINGS ...
...THE FEELINGS I'D ALWAYS PRETENDED NOT TO NOTICE.
WE'LL SEE EACH OTHER AGAIN ONE DAY, RIGHT?
THE HERO TATSUO LOOKED UP TO...
YES!
...WAS NOTHING BUT A LYING COWARD.

IF YOU CAN'T RUN, TATSUO, I'LL DO THE RUNNING! I'LL DO THE FIGHTING!
YOU'LL BE THE BRAINS, AND I'LL BE THE BODY!
YOU AND I ARE SEPARATE BUT ONE! WE'RE BOTH DRAGONS—TEAM MIRACLE DRAGON!
WE'RE A DRAGON—WE CAN'T BE SPLIT APART!
AS LONG AS WE'RE TOGETHER—YOU CAN BE A HERO, TATSUO! YOU COULD SAVE THE WORLD!
I WAS ALWAYS FULL OF BLUSTER IN FRONT OF TATSUO.
I'M THE CAPTAIN, RIGHT?
MIRACLE DRAGON... A BRAG FROM A WIMP WHO COULDN'T EVEN DO A PULLOVER.
HIRYU, DON'T FORGET ME AFTER YOU MOVE!
WHAT'RE YOU TALKING ABOUT? OF COURSE I'LL NEVER FORGET YOU!
HIRYU, I MADE THIS FOR YOU...

DO YOU REMEMBER, TATSUO?
BACK WHEN YOU WERE STRUGGLING TO RIDE A BICYCLE...
DON'T CRY, TATSUO!
I WANTED TO BE A SUPERHERO FOR YOU.
WAAH! I'M PROBABLY THE ONLY GRADE-SCHOOLER ON EARTH WHO WIPED OUT ON A BIKE WITH TRAINING WHEELS!
DON'T TAKE IT SO HARD! I'M SURE THERE ARE PLENTY!
HOW WOULD YOU KNOW, HIRYU? YOU'VE ONLY BEEN ALIVE EIGHT YEARS!
YEAH, WELL, THAT'S ONE YEAR LONGER THAN YOU!
NOW MY LEG TREMORS ARE STARTING AGAIN. I GUESS I'LL GO HOME.
OH, C'MON! SO WHAT? I THOUGHT YOU WANTED TO BE A HERO, TATSUO!
I KNOW THAT'S JUST A DREAM. FORGET IT.
!
I JUST WANTED TO BE ABLE TO RIDE SOME-WHERE FAR AWAY TOGETHER ON OUR BIKES...
DON'T TALK LIKE THAT!

HE'S...
...NUTS!
OBORO MOCHIZUKI... AN AIRHEAD ACTOR WITH MORE THAN A FEW SCREWS LOOSE!
THE LAST GUY ON EARTH YOU WANT TO ENTRUST YOUR LIFE TO!
SORRY, GUYS! I COULDN'T STOP HIM!!
WELL, GOOD LUCK, EVERYONE!
...
EVER SINCE MY FEVER SUBSIDED...
...I FEEL STRANGELY ENERGIZED!
IT'S LIKE SOME SORT OF POWER WELLING UP DEEP IN MY BRAIN!
I FEEL LIKE A GOD!
GO FORTH, OBORO!!

YOU DON'T GET IT. IT'S TOTALLY NOT A MATTER OF PRIDE!
THIS IS A MATTER OF THE SOUL!
IT'S SIMPLY NOT *ME* TO SIT BACK AND WATCH WHEN DANGER ABOUNDS.
INSATIABLE CURIOSITY-THAT'S *ME*!
YES...
...THIS IS DESTINY!
AH ...
AAAUGH!
YIKES!

WAI-
WAI-
WAIT...
YOU'RE GOING?! WHATTAYA MEAN, YOU'RE GOING?!
I'M GOING WITH THEM.
I WON'T LET THEM LEAVE ME OUT! IT'S NOT FAIR!
HUH?! NOT FAIR?!
YEAH! I WANNA DO SOMETHING TOO!

I BET IF HE GETS ONE GOOD ENHANCE PUNCH IN, I'LL BE OUT COLD.
PREPARE FOR THE FIGHT OF YOUR LIFE, AGEHA YOSHINA!
VWWW
VSH
BRING IT ON!
BOOOM

ALL RIGHT!!
QUIT MESSIN' WITH THAT THING AND COME DOWN HERE!
VWHOOO
HOW 'BOUT A LITTLE ONE-ON-ONE, TATSUO?
DOINK
GOOD.
IF YOU'RE NOT ALMOST PISSING YOUR PANTS...
...IT AIN'T A REAL FIGHT!

...MF!
ZING
I KNEW I'D REGRET USING TRANCE AND ENHANCE AT THE SAME TIME...
MORE TIME...
I NEED MORE TIME!
VWHOoo
I FEEL...
FWAH
...AWESOME!

RRRMBLE
THAT'S RIGHT. GOOD BOY.
THIS WAY!
CALL.21: BAIT
PHEW ...
TMP

POW

TATSUOOOOO!!

IT'S STARTING!
KLANG
KLANG
...
KLANG
KLANG

YOSHINA !!
YOU'RE NOT THE ONLY ONE WHO CARES ABOUT SAVING AN OLD FRIEND... *HIRYU!*

9:30 P.M.

COME ALONG ...

KLANG
LET'S GO FOR A LITTLE WALK, WORM!
VWISH
KLANG
KLANG
SHING
SHING

BY THE WAY...
...ABOUT THE PLAN YOU PROPOSED...
WHAT?
YOU AGREED! I THOUGHT WE'D SETTLED THIS!
YOU SAID YOU'D APPROACH HIM FROM THE FRONT...
AND WHILE HE'S DISTRACTED, I'M SUPPOSED TO CIRCLE AROUND...
...AND CUT HIM OFF FROM THE SIDE!!
TATSUO
ME
YOU
BUT DOESN'T THAT PRETTY MUCH JUST MAKE YOU BAIT?
THAT'S RIGHT! WE'RE GONNA LET HIM THINK I'M THE ONLY IDIOT WHO CAME RUNNING ACROSS THIS CURSED WASTELAND BEGGING TO GET SHOT!
I'M THE BAIT. HE KNOWS ENHANCE! THE WHOLE PLAN RIDES ON YOU, HIRYU!
YOU IDIOT! DON'T YOU REALIZE HOW MUCH DANGER YOU'RE PUTTING YOURSELF IN?
YOU WANT TO SAVE TATSUO, DON'T YOU?
WHAT?
I KNOW WHAT AMAMIYA SAID, BUT YOU HAVEN'T GIVEN UP HOPE, HAVE YOU?
YOU WANT TO BRING TATSUO BACK TO HIS SENSES—AND BRING HIM BACK WITH US TO THE PRESENT, RIGHT?
THUMP
WELL THEN, I'LL DO EVERYTHING I CAN TO HELP YOU.
EVEN IF I WIND UP IN A TIGHT CORNER—I TRUST YOU TO HANDLE IT!

IF YOU GET YOUR-SELVES KILLED...
...I'M GOING TO BE SUPER PISSED!
VWHSH
WOW, THAT WAS REALLY ...
... TOUCH-ING.
YEAH.
SHALL WE?
YEAH.
SHIP
9:23 P.M.

OKAY, BUT WE CAN'T TAKE YOU WITH US, CAN WE?
YEAH!
NO FAIR!
I WANNA COME TOO!
GROW UP!
TAKING CARE OF SICK PEOPLE IS AN IMPORTANT JOB.
WE NEED YOU TO TAKE CARE OF KABUTO KIRISAKI.
HUH?
FWHOO
ALL RIGHT, YOU TWO, DON'T FORGET WHAT I TOLD YOU.
GOT IT.
DO YOUR STUFF, AMA-MIYA!
WHSH
?

WE'LL MAKE OUR MOVE AT 9:30.
UNTIL THEN, WE'LL GET AS MUCH REST AS WE CAN.
RIGHT!
HEY, HIRYU...
CAN I TALK TO YOU A SEC?
WHAT'S UP?
VWHSHH
CURRENT TIME IN PRESENT-DAY JAPAN: 9:15 P.M.
HEY! HOW COME I HAVE TO WAIT HERE WITH KIRISAKI?
HUH?
IT'S MY PLAN! I WANT TO HELP!

HIS GUN'S AT ABOUT 50%.
HE'S REFUELING A LOT SLOWER THIS TIME.
...
HE'S BEEN LEANING ON HIS PSIONIC POWERS PRETTY HEAVILY TOO, SO IT STANDS TO REASON HE'S SLOWING DOWN.
LUCKY FOR US. NOW WE CAN REST OUR BRAINS TOO.
VWHSHH
ACCORDING TO OUR CELL PHONES, THE PRESENT-DAY TIME IS EIGHT O'CLOCK... I'D ESTIMATE HE TOOK ABOUT TWO-AND-A-HALF HOURS TO RELOAD LAST TIME.
AND THIS TIME?
THIS TIME, HE STARTED RELOADING AROUND SIX... AFTER TWO HOURS, HIS ENERGY'S STILL ONLY AT AROUND 50%.
SO HE PROBABLY WON'T FINISH 'TIL AROUND TEN O'CLOCK.
20:00

I THINK I CAN LAST A PRETTY LONG TIME IF I JUST USE ENHANCE TO TRAVEL BETWEEN SAFE SPOTS, RESTING BETWEEN.
I CAN PROBABLY EARN US 20 OR 30 MINUTES. OF COURSE, IT ALL DEPENDS ON OUR LUCK...
VWHOOO

THE SKY'S STARTING TO GET DARK.
DON'T WORRY. IT DOESN'T GET ANY DARKER THAN THIS.
PER-SISTENT LITTLE BUGGER, AIN'T IT?
YOU THINK IT'D MAKE GOOD EATIN'?
DON'T GO OUT TOO FAR-YOU'LL ATTRACT ITS ATTENTION AGAIN!
I'LL PUNCH IT RIGHT IN THE FACE!
DON'T BE A MORON!
RUMBLERUMBLE
ALL RIGHT— IT'S ALL YOURS, AMAMIYA.
YEP. I'LL DISTRACT IT AND GET IT TO CHASE ME.
AMAMIYA BEGRUDG-INGLY AGREED TO OBORO'S PLAN.
NONE OF THE REST OF US COULD PULL A STUNT LIKE THAT ANYWAY.
AMA-MIYA'S THE ONLY ONE FOR THE JOB.

...
THEY BOTH SEEM PRETTY DETER-MINED.
WHAT DO YOU SAY, AMA MIYA?
HUMPH.
FINE. HAVE IT YOUR WAY.
That's right, baby! Uh-huh!
OH, DEAR.
GRRRR
VWHOOO
CURRENT TIME IN PRESENT-DAY JAPAN: 7:55 P.M.
YOWCH!
SHANK
HIRYU...

B-BUT ...
I-I-IT'S DANGER-OUS!
IT'S R-REALLY ROUGH OUT THERE !!
EVEN IF YOU WEREN'T TIRED...
I'D NEVER LET YOU GO.
I'M DONE WITH THAT.
I DON'T EVER WANT TO JUST SIT THERE ...
...TWIDDLING MY THUMBS AND MAKING EXCUSES TO MYSELF WHILE YOU FIGHT.
NEVER AGAIN.
THIS TIME, I WANT TO BE ON THE FRONT LINE.
LEAVE THE FIGHTING TO US. WE'RE SPECIAL-ISTS!
THIS TIME, I'M GOING TO BE THE ONE PROTECT-ING AMAMIYA!

ALL RIGHT— I'LL GO WITH YOU, HIRYU.
THEN YOU WON'T HAVE TO WORRY, RIGHT, AMAMIYA?
YOSHINA!
THAT'S THE OPPOSITE OF RE-ASSURING! GET IT!?
SCRUNCH
SCRUNCH
SCRUNCH
HNFRA FRGH! WHY??
LOOK, I'VE MADE UP MY MIND! I'M GOING WITH HIRYU!
DON'T BE A FOOL!
YOU'RE THE FOOL!
YOU WANNA GET YOURSELF KILLED PROTECTING US?!
!
I KNOW YOU'RE TRYING TO ACT ALL TOUGH, BUT ANY IDIOT CAN SEE HOW EXHAUSTED YOU ARE FROM THE PSI YOU'VE ALREADY USED!
!
OOF
THERE'S NO WAY WE'RE LETTING YOU GO UP AGAINST THAT DUDE OR THAT WORM AGAIN TO PROTECT US!
I NEVER WANT TO SEE YOU ALL SHREDDED LIKE THAT AGAIN!

ASA-GA ...
I'LL GET THE MASK.
I HAVE TO DO THIS MYSELF.
SLAM
I NEED TO SETTLE THINGS BETWEEN US.
THAT'S FINE. I WON'T TRY TO STOP YOU.
YOU SEEM ABLE TO USE THIS "PSI" POWER, TOO...
I DON'T GET WHY ANYONE WOULD BE SO HOT TO FACE OFF WITH A TRIGGER-HAPPY MANIAC ...
WE'LL NEED TO MAKE OUR MOVE BEFORE TATSUO FINISHES RELOAD-ING.
WE DON'T WANT HIM SHOOTING THAT BEAST OF A GUN AT US AGAIN.
BUT...
TATSUO DOESN'T JUST USE BLAST...
HE USES ENHANCE TOO!

VWHOOO
WE'RE GOING TO STEAL TATSUO'S MASK?
THAT BLACK FACE MASK HE'S WEARING?
YEP. THAT'S THE ONE.
IT SEEMS IT PRODUCES SOUND WAVES THAT REPEL THE GIANT WORM THAT PLAGUES US.
ONCE WE GET OUR HANDS ON IT, WE'LL BE ABLE TO MAKE IT TO THE GATE.
I'M NOT SURE... THE WORM DID SEEM TO RUN AWAY WHEN HE MADE THAT SOUND...
WELL, IF WE DON'T TRY SOMETHING WE'LL NEVER GET HOME, RIGHT?
WE'VE GOT TO TAKE ACTION BEFORE HE ATTACKS AGAIN.
I GUESS WE CAN TRY.
QUESTION IS HOW... WITH THAT WORM ON THE LOOSE, WE'RE STUCK.
RIGHT. WE NEED TO DISTRACT THE WORM.
THE OTHER TEAM CAN SNEAK UP AND GRAB THE MASK.
THEN I WANT TO BE THE ONE TO APPROACH TATSUO!
I WON'T TAKE NO FOR AN ANSWER!

TWO HOURS EARLIER ...
HAHH
SHFF
HAHH
AROUND 7:30, PRESENT-DAY JAPAN TIME...
HAHH
HAHH
HE'S NO LONGER THE TATSUO YOU ONCE KNEW.
HE'S A TABOO.
HIS MIND AND MEMORIES ARE ALMOST COMPLETELY GONE.
I DON'T THINK THE OLD TATSUO IS EVER COMING BACK.
HIRYU, WE NEED TO TALK. COME JOIN US.
ALL RIGHT.
...

CALL.20: OPERATION

HERE I COME!!
OM

THE TIME IN PRESENT-DAY JAPAN IS 9:31 P.M.
ALL RIGHT!
21:31
BEEP BEEP BEEP BEEP
HERE GOES NOTHING!
SHOOP
AGEHA REACHES THE BOTTOM OF THE CLIFF...
GOOD... THE WORM'S NOWHERE TO BE SEEN.
CALL.20: OPERATION
OKAY... HERE GOES !!
I'VE JUST GOT TO TRUST AMAMIYA... AND HIRYU...

AAAAUGH

AFTER THAT, AMAMIYA LAY DOWN AND HAD A REST.
AS SHE REPLEN-ISHED HER STRENGTH FOR THE NEXT BATTLE...
...SHE SILENTLY BORE THE PHYSICAL AND MENTAL STRAIN BROUGHT ON BY SUSTAINED PSI USE.
WE HAD ONE TOTALLY SPENT GIRL, TWO SICK DUDES...
EVERY-THING'S SPIN-NING!
MY HEAD'S SPIN-NING!
...AND ONE GUY WHO HADN'T SPOKEN A WORD SINCE HIS CONVERSATION WITH AMAMIYA WHEN SHE GOT BACK.
THINGS WERE LOOKING PRETTY BLEAK...
...AND WE STILL WEREN'T ANY CLOSER TO FIGURING OUT HOW TO GET TO THAT GATE.
YOSHINA...
CAN WE TALK?
HOW-EVER...
...EVERY-THING TOOK A TURN FOR THE BETTER WHEN OBORO MOCHIZUKI RECOVERED.

I'M BACK.
SHF
HA!
YOU HAD US WORRIED, STUPID!
YOU SHOULDN'T HAVE DONE THAT!
ZING
...

GYOW
KKRASH
...
RUMBLERUMBLE
WHERE'S AMAMIYA?! WHAT HAPPENED TO HER?!
...

SHE'S TRYING TO DRAW HIS FIRE!

VVVOOSH
WATCH OUT! GET OUT OF THERE!!
KACHUNG
COME ON...
COME ON!...
KA-CHUNK

HE KNOWS HE'S WEAK.
HE'S OWNING UP TO IT HONESTLY—
WITH A SORT OF GRACEFUL STRENGTH ...
HIS EMOTIONS BLAZE WHITE HOT...
...SOMETIMES PRODUCING DAZZLING TONGUES OF FIRE.
HE'S HOLDING HIMSELF BACK...
...CURSING HIS OWN HELPLESS-NESS...
RIGHT NOW, OUR LIVES ALL DEPEND ...
...ON JUST ONE YOUNG GIRL...

ARGH... THAT AMAMIYA! THIS IS TOO DANGER-OUS!
WAIT! WHAT GOOD'LL IT DO FOR YOU TO GO AFTER HER?!
THE ONLY THING WE CAN DO RIGHT NOW IS DISTANCE OURSELVES FROM THE BIGGEST TARGET—THAT BUILDING—AND KEEP REPOSITIONING OURSELVES IN SPOTS WHERE WE'RE HARD TO HIT.
THESE OTHER TWO ARE HELPLESS! IF HE FIRES OVER HERE AND YOU AND I AREN'T HERE, WHAT'LL HAPPEN TO THEM?
BESIDES, IF WE GO OUT THERE, AMAMIYA WILL JUST TRY TO PROTECT US!!
UNK
DAMN !!
I HATE TO SAY IT, BUT THE BEST THING WE CAN DO FOR AMAMIYA IS STAY PUT!
THIS BOY...

CHSH
HAHH
VROO
HAHH
OH NO!
THAT MONSTER'S BACK IN ACTION TOO!
SHOOM
AMAMIYA ?!
HAHH
HAHH
THAT GUY STILL HAS ONE SHOT LEFT!
AMAMIYA STILL ISN'T READY TO CALL IT QUITS!

VWWWSH
TO HAVE DEVELOPED SUCH DEXTERITY IN A BODY THAT WAS ONCE DISABLED...
HE'S NOT JUST A BLASTER BUT A SKILLED ENHANCER TOO!
THIRD BLAST ...

THIS PERSON IS NO LONGER ...
EN-HANCE!
... TATSUO...
FWAM
SHWOO

GET UP! AMA-MIYA !!
BOOM
C'MON, AMAMIYA!! GET UP!!
YES.
YES, I KNOW.

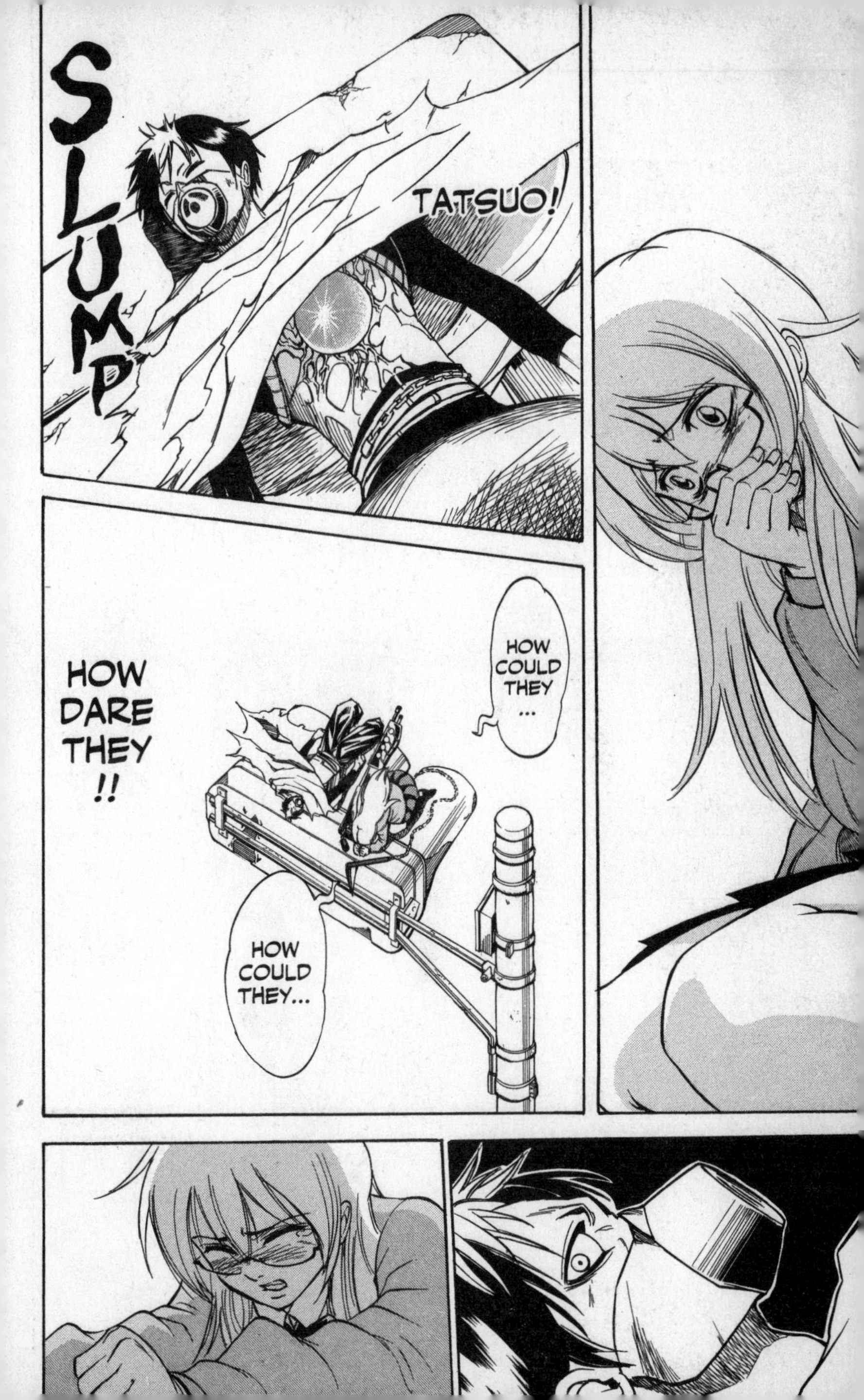
SLUMP
TATSUO!
HOW COULD THEY ...
HOW COULD THEY...
HOW DARE THEY !!

WAIT... IS THAT... A TABOO NUCLEUS?!
VHRRRR
OH NO!
NOOO!! STOP!!
AAAAUGH !!

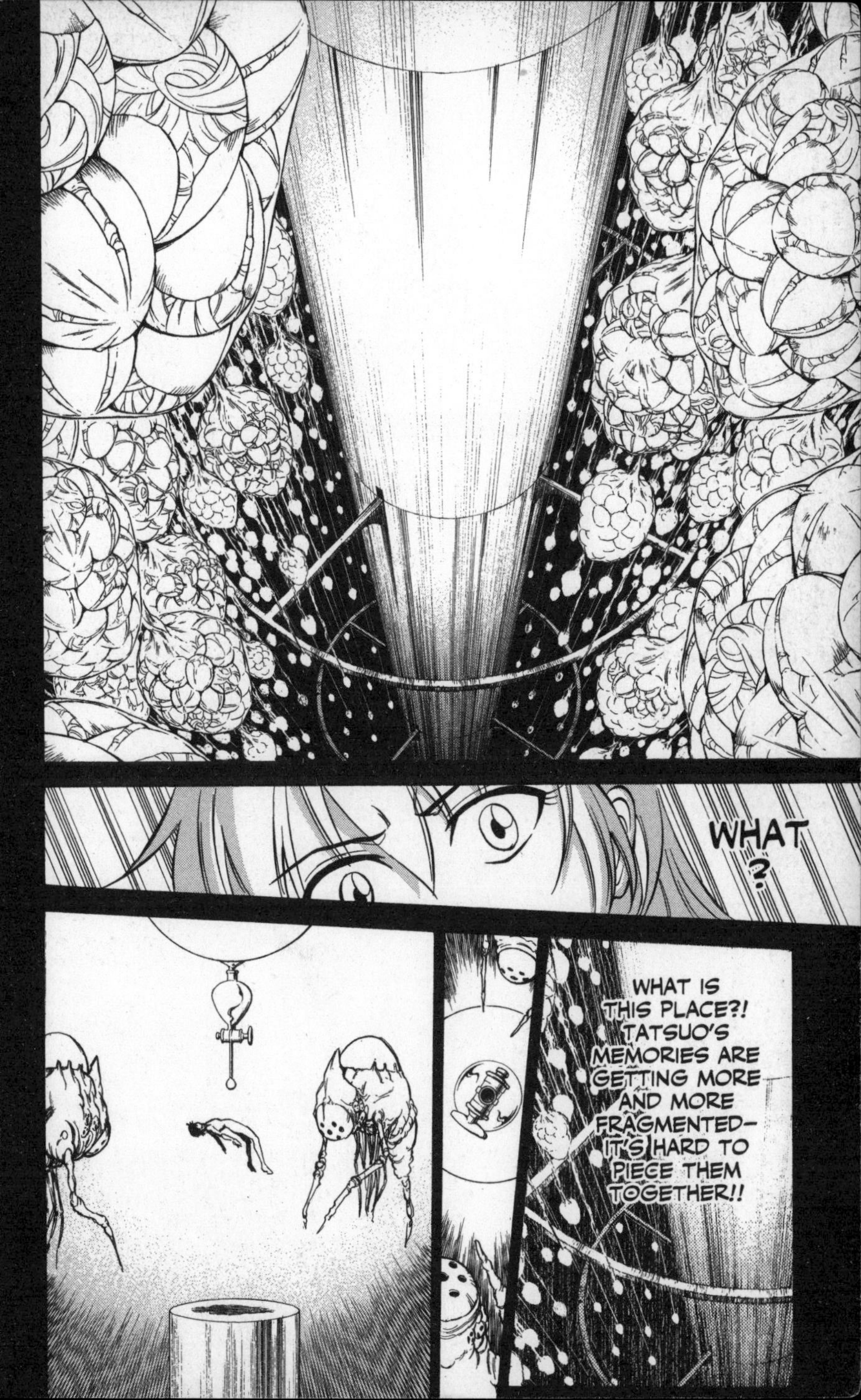
WHAT ?
WHAT IS THIS PLACE?! TATSUO'S MEMORIES ARE GETTING MORE AND MORE FRAGMENTED—IT'S HARD TO PIECE THEM TOGETHER!!

STOP! LET ME GO!
WHERE ARE YOU TAKING ME?!
KRACKLE KRACKLE
THE TABOO CAPTURED HIM AND CARRIED HIM AWAY!
WHERE TO?
DON'T TELL ME...
A PSYREN TOWER !?

THESE ARE... FRAGMENTS OF TATSUO'S MEMORY!
GET UP! RUN AWAY! RUN!!
LUB-DUB
LUB-DUB
DAMN IT— WHY WON'T MY BODY EVER DO WHAT I TELL IT TO?!
I NEVER IMAGINED PSYREN WOULD BE SUCH A HORRIBLE PLACE! I SHOULD NEVER HAVE COME, ASAGA!
SO IT REALLY IS TATSUO MANA, ASAGA'S FRIEND WHO DISAPPEARED INTO PSYREN! BUT WHAT BECAME OF HIM AFTER THAT?

CALL. 19:
THE YOUNG GIRL, THE TABOO, AND THE BROKEN HEART
WHAT A CONFUSED MIND. NO MATTER HOW FAR I DIVE, ALL I FIND IS DARKNESS.
HUMAN FUNCTION IS IMPOSSIBLE IN THIS KIND OF MENTAL STATE!
LIKE THE MIND OF SOMEONE IN A DEEP COMA...
SHWOOO
I DOVE INTO A MIND LIKE THIS ONCE BEFORE...
LONG AGO-THE MIND OF A TABOO MONSTER!
!!
A LIGHT...
THERE! THE FAINT TRACES OF RESIDUAL CON-SCIOUS-NESS...

CONNECTION ESTAB-LISHED!
VWSH
INITIATING MIND DIVE AT 2,000 FM/M...
WHSHH

CALL.19: THE YOUNG GIRL, THE TABOO, AND THE BROKEN HEART

★ Call 19!
★ Right this way!
Amamiya?

SHO
TRANCE!
WHO ARE YOU— PERPLEXING ASAGA SO?
FWOM
I'M GOING TO HAVE A LITTLE PEEK INSIDE YOUR MIND.
WIRED MIND JACK!

VWSH
KSHING
WOOSH
!!
TWO SHOTS!
BLAM
BLAM

IT'S MY
TURN TO
PROTECT
YOU TWO!

!!

SPEED: OVER-DRIVE!
KA-BOOM

FWHOOOOO
VWHOO
THE TWO OF YOU ...
... SAVED MY LIFE.
YOU SAVED ME.
ENHANCE.
ALL MOTOR NERVES, ACTIVATE!
COME TO THINK OF IT, I DON'T CRY ANYMORE AT HOME NOW.

AMAMIYA! WHAT'RE YOU GOING TO DO?!
WHEN THOSE GUYS GOT SICK, I KNEW I'D HAVE TO DO THIS.
DON'T WORRY.
I'M USED TO FIGHTING.
...!!
I HAVE AN IDEA.
YOU TWO CAN'T USE ENHANCE— YOU'D JUST GET IN MY WAY.
IF YOU'RE REALLY WORRIED ABOUT ME...
...JUST MAKE SURE YOU PROTECT THOSE TWO.
DON'T BE A FOOL!

RUMBLERUMBLE
HE'S DONE RE-LOADING!
THAT WAS WAY QUICKER ...
... THAN I EX-PECTED!
WHAT ?!
YOSHINA AND ASAGA! YOU TWO STAY HERE AND PROTECT THE OTHERS!
KA-SHING
DON'T TRY TO COUNTER HIS BLAST ATTACKS! FOCUS ON GETTING OUT OF THE WAY!

CHILL OUT, BRO!
CHOMP
CHOMP
BEATING YOUR HEAD AGAINST THE WALL ISN'T GOING TO GET YOU ANY ANSWERS, RIGHT, DRAGON? ♪
WHAT'RE YOU DOING?
ME? I'M NOURISHING MY BOD AND RESTING MY BRAIN.
THERE'S NO TELLING WHAT'S GONNA HAPPEN, BUT WE'RE UP AGAINST A PSIONIST.
WE'LL NEED TO BE IN PEAK CONDITION!
I ENVY YOUR SIMPLE-MINDED-NESS.
HA HA!
FINE, I'M SIMPLE-MINDED.
IT'S BETTER THAN BEING DELICATE.
YOU LITTLE PUNK! I BOUGHT THAT SANDWICH AND MILK, MAN!
SHUT UP! IT'S ALL MINE! THERE'S NO MILK IN THIS WORLD FOR YOU! NONE!
WHAP
WHAP
AT LEAST THEY'RE ENER-GETIC...
VWHOO
OH NO!

RRRR...
KRK
UNH!!
BAM
WHO ARE YOU?!
THAT GAZE... THAT FACE...
THE MORE I DENY IT, THE MORE I'M CONVINCED IT'S TRUE.
...HOW COULD IT BE ANYONE ELSE?
ASAGA ...
TATSUO MANA...
WHY ARE YOU DOING THIS?!
DUDE, YOU'VE GOTTA GET A GRIP!

YEEKS!
CHILLY!
JUST TAKE IT EASY. YOU'LL FEEL BETTER SOON.
THANK YOU!
MY ANGEL!
SELFISH JERK!
EXCUSE ME, FRIENDS... I'M TERRIBLY SORRY FOR MY DEPLORABLE ATTITUDE JUST MOMENTS AGO...
LET'S JUST START OVER AND GIVE THIS SOME THOUGHT... I'M SURE THERE'S A WAY ALL FIVE OF US CAN MAKE IT...
YOU CAN CALL ME KABUTO, OR KABU, IF YOU PREFER.
LET'S BE FRIENDS, 'KAY?
YOU'VE GOT SOME NERVE!!
RRRUMBLE RUMBLE

OH, YEAH? I WILL, THEN!
IF I HAVE TO TIP-TOE THE WHOLE WAY, OR CRAWL ON ALL FOURS, EVEN... I'LL GET TO THAT GATE ON MY OWN! JUST WATCH ME!
SKSH
WHEN IT COMES TO RUNNING AWAY, HIDING AND APOLOGIZING, AIN'T NOBODY GOT ME BEAT, BRO–
?! HA... ROOO ?
?!
WOBBLE
WHUD
HEY!
DON'T TELL ME...
YA?
HAHH
HAHH
...HE'S AWAKENING TOO?!
!!
NOW WE'RE REALLY STUCK!

SNATCH
?
HRK?
DANGLE
HAROOOOOO!
TOSS
YOU'D BETTER WATCH IT, MAN!
GRRR
YEAH, JUST WATCH IT!
WHAT THE HECK, MAN?!
THAT'S THE MOST WORKED UP I'VE SEEN YOU DUDES!
SO...
...WHAT SHOULD WE DO?
HUMPH! HOW'RE WE SUPPOSED TO DO ANYTHING IF WE HAFTA LOOK AFTER A SICK GUY?!
NOW WE'RE ALL GONNA DIE!
FINE! WHY DON'T YOU JUST FEND FOR YOURSELF, THEN?
I DON'T GIVE A SNOT WHAT HAPPENS TO YOU!

HUH?
LOOK—THE LIGHT'S FILLING UP EVENLY IN ALL FOUR GAUGES!
IT'S KINDA HARD TO SEE, BUT...
...YOU SEE IT, RIGHT?
I DON'T THINK IT WOULD FILL UP THAT WAY IF HE COULD CHARGE UP ONE SHOT AT A TIME.
YOU'RE RIGHT! GOOD EYE!
I KNOW, RIGHT?
WHSHH
WHENEVER YOU'RE IN TROUBLE, JUST CALL ON ME, LITTLE BUNNY!
OOF
I MAY NOT LOOK LIKE IT, BUT I KNOW HOW TO TAKE CARE OF A GIRL.
N'EST-CE PAS?
WHO ARE YOU?!

THE QUESTION IS, HOW LONG WILL IT TAKE HIM TO RELOAD?
HOW LONG DO WE HAVE BEFORE HIS NEXT ATTACK?
I THINK THAT GUN OF HIS FIRES FOUR SHOTS. THOSE LIGHTS ON THE BARREL ALL WENT OUT AFTER HE FIRED FOUR TIMES.
I'M GUESSING THAT'S THE MAXIMUM AMOUNT OF PSI HE CAN LOAD INTO THERE!
BUT WAIT! SAY HIS GUN DOES HOLD FOUR SHOTS...
THERE'S NO GUARAN-TEEING HE'LL LOAD UP ALL FOUR!
HE COULD SHOOT US AS SOON AS HE'S GOT ONE BLAST READY TO GO!
IF SO, HE MIGHT ATTACK AT ANY MOMENT!
RIGHT ...
FWHOO
NO...
I THINK HE'S GOTTA CHARGE UP ALL FOUR BEFORE HE CAN SHOOT.

...
I'M WITH AGEHA.
LET'S COME UP WITH A WAY TO SAVE ALL FIVE OF US.
VWHOOO
HOW LONG DO YOU THINK IT'LL TAKE FOR MOCHIZUKI'S SYMPTOMS TO PASS?
WELL, IT VARIES FROM PERSON TO PERSON, BUT PROBABLY TWO OR THREE HOURS. I JUST HOPE IT HAPPENS BEFORE THAT GUY STARTS SHOOTING AGAIN...
AS LONG WE'RE STUCK HERE...
...HIS LONG-DISTANCE BLAST ATTACK IS GOING TO BE A REAL PROBLEM.

FWHOO
I SAY WE GOT NO CHOICE. IF THE DUDE'S TOO SICK TO MOVE, WE'VE GOTTA LEAVE HIM HERE.
LET'S JUST FIGURE OUT HOW THE REST OF US ARE GONNA GET TO THIS GATE THING.
WHAT'S WRONG WITH YOU? WHAT KIND OF LOWLIFE COULD DO A THING LIKE THAT?!
THE NAME'S KABUTO KIRISAKI! CALL ME KIRISAKI!
WHAT I'M SAYING IS, IF WE DRAG OUR FEET, THAT MANIAC'S GONNA BLAST US AGAIN!
AND IF WE VENTURE OUT THERE DRAGGING A SICK GUY ALONG, WE'RE GONNA BE WORM FOOD FROM THE GET-GO!
THAT'S NOT HOW I WANNA DIE!
YEAH, BUT YOU'RE TALKING ABOUT ABAN-DONING HIM TO HIS DEATH!
I'M NOT DOWN WITH THAT!

Call. 18: My Turn

I'M HOT ...
HAHHH
HAHHH
AAAAUGH! MY NECK!! HE TOUCHED MY NECK!!!
PLEASE... STAY WITH ME...I NEED SOMEONE TO HELP ME WHEN I'M SICK...
AAAAUGH! LET GO OF ME!
WE NEED A PLAN.
THIS IS GOING TO MAKE IT THAT MUCH HARDER FOR THE FIVE OF US TO MAKE OUR MOVE.
QUIT PANTING ON ME!!
I REFUSE TO BELIEVE ...
... THAT'S TATSUO !!

MOCHI-ZUKI!!
WUMP
CALL. 18: MY TURN
HIS POWERS ARE COMING ONLINE!
THE PSIONIC DOORS IN HIS MIND ARE OPENING!
THE HIGH FEVER AND NOSE-BLEED HIT HIM WAY FASTER THAN IT HIT US!
HUH? WHAT? COMING ONLINE?! WHADDYA MEAN?!
THIS IS BAD!
SERIOUSLY BAD TIMING!
!!
SHP

Without further ado...
...we bring you Call.18: My Turn!
SHWAP

READ THIS WAY
SHLIP
?!
WHAT'S UP? THAT'S A SERIOUS NOSEBLEED, MAN!
WOBBLE
I'M FINE.
I'M JUST KIND OF COLD ...

WE HAVE TO...
...FIGHT HIM.
WE MIGHT HAVE TO...
WHAT?!
BEFORE HE FINISHES LOADING, WE HAVE TO FIND A WAY...
...FOR THE FIVE OF US TO DEFEAT A PSIONIST OPPONENT, CROSS A WASTELAND WITH A GIANT MONSTER WORM, AND REACH THE GATE!

WHAT'S WITH THAT FREAKY DUDE?
UM, HE'S TRYING TO KILL US...
NO!
I HAVE NO IDEA WHAT THIS SAI STUFF IS...
BUT, LIKE, HOW MUCH TIME DO WE HAVE LEFT BEFORE THAT MANIAC STARTS FIRING ON US AGAIN?!
I DON'T KNOW HOW POWERFUL HIS ABILITIES ARE...
...BUT FOR AN ATTACK OF THAT MAGNITUDE, I'LL BET IT TAKES SOME TIME.
THEN LET'S GET OUT OF HERE NOW!
TO WHERE?
THIS WHOLE PLACE IS A GIANT WORM HUNTING GROUND!
PLUS, THAT TATSUO LOOKALIKE IS BETWEEN US AND THE GATE THAT TAKES US HOME!

WHAP
TUNK
NWAH
WHAT'S THE DEAL?
HE'S JUST SITTING THERE. ISN'T HE GOING TO SHOOT AT US AGAIN?
MAYBE HE'S OUT OF AMMO?
I GET IT. HIS BLAST ENERGY POWERS THAT GUN.
HE HAS TO REFUEL IT WITH HIS PSI BEFORE HE CAN ATTACK AGAIN.

RUMBLE RUMBLE
KLIK
...
KSHHH
BAMBAMBAM
I THOUGHT WE WERE GONERS!
GOOD THING WE WEREN'T HIGHER UP.
TALK ABOUT BLIND LUCK!
YOU OKAY?
YEAH.

KA-BOOM
!!
KA-KRASH

!!!
WHY'D YOU CALL OUT TO HIM!? ARE YOU NUTS?!
WATCH OUT!!
!
BLAM
BLAM

IT RAN AWAY?!
PHOOEY! WIMPY WORM!
SOME-THING FREAKED IT OUT!
THAT SOUND!! IT CAME FROM THAT GUY'S MASK!!
TATSUO!!
YOU'RE ALIVE!! IS IT REALLY YOU!?
KA-CHA

YEAH! GET HIM! EAT HIM UP!!
PHWEEEEET
SHHHP
SKREEE
?!

!!
BOOOO-
HE'S A BLASTER !!
OOM
KA-BOOM
LOOK! THE MONSTER'S HEADED STRAIGHT FOR HIM!!
VWHOOOM

STOP
!!

HUNH
SHMP
!
THAT ...
VSHOO

HEY! THERE'S STILL ONE GUY LEFT!
KOFF
NNGHH
KSHHH

THEN I'LL WALK AT YOUR PACE.
THAT'S WHAT I TOLD HIM.
ASAGA ...
... WHY DID I...
LET'S GO TO PSYREN TO-GETHER!
BUT THEN ...
"I'M NOT GOING, TATSUO."
... REFUSE HIM?

OH...

WHAT DO I DO NOW?

WHAT CAN I TELL HIS FAMILY?

DON'T EVEN TRY. HOW CAN YOU EXPLAIN? THERE'S NOT MUCH WE CAN TELL THEM.

FWSHH

HE TOLD ME IT WAS ALWAYS SO HARD FOR HIM, TRYING TO KEEP UP WITH EVERYONE...

HE COULDN'T EVEN RUN... THE OLDER HE GOT, THE MORE IT FRUSTRATED HIM...

I'M SORRY ...
I DID SEE TATSUO IN PSYREN.
BUT SOME-WHERE ALONG THE WAY, HE DISAP-PEARED.
I'M GUESSING HE WAS KILLED.

DO YOU RECOGNIZE THIS FACE? HIS NAME'S TATSUO MANA.
HE WAS A GRADE BELOW ME IN SCHOOL. HE DISAPPEARED INTO PSYREN.
TATSUO WAS DISABLED— HE SUFFERED FROM PHYSICAL PROBLEMS SINCE BIRTH.
HE COULDN'T DO A LOT OF THE THINGS HE WANTED TO, AND HE MISSED A LOT OF SCHOOL.
WE WERE NEIGHBORS BACK IN GRADE SCHOOL, SO I STOPPED BY TO SEE HIM A LOT.
SINCE HE COULDN'T PLAY OUTSIDE, I TOLD HIM STORIES INSTEAD. ABOUT HITTING A HOME RUN, OR FIGHTING OFF A WILD DOG...
ALL LIES, OF COURSE.
YOU REMEMBER. I WAS A TOTAL WIMP MYSELF!
YOU'RE SO COOL, HIRYU!
I JUST GOT A KICK OUT OF MAKING HIM SMILE.

BLAST...
FWAH
IT'S AN AMAZING POWER. DON'T YOU THINK SO, AMAMIYA?
SCRUNCH
KRUNCH
ANYONE WITHOUT TRAINING IN PSI WOULD HAVE NO IDEA WHAT I JUST DID.
IT'S ACTUALLY LIKE THE INVISIBLE HAND OF A GOD!
BUT I WANT A STRONGER IMAGE THAN A HAND...
BE CAREFUL. IN A BATTLE BETWEEN PSIONISTS, DEPENDING ON THE SKILL OF THE COMBATANTS, SOMETIMES YOU CAN'T SEE EACH OTHER'S PSI.
FREEZ

READ THIS WAY

TATSUO ?!
I'M NOT AFTER THE REWARD.
I WAS SEARCHING FOR SOMEONE, AND I WOUND UP HERE.
I'M LOOKING FOR TATSUO, A YOUNGER GUY I WENT TO SCHOOL WITH WHO GOT A PSYREN PHONE CARD AND DISAPPEARED. CAN ANYONE TELL ME ANYTHING?

WHAT?! WHAT'S HE DOING HERE?
DON'T TELL ME... HE SURVIVED THIS WHOLE TIME?!
HOLD ON! WHAT'S GOING ON?
YOU KNOW HIM TOO, AMAMIYA ?

...
IS THAT TRIGGER-HAPPY MANIAC A FRIEND OF YOURS?!
HIRYU !!
HOW'S YOSHINA'S TRAINING GOING?
OH, HE'S AS OUT-OF-CONTROL AS EVER!

FWSHHH
VWHOOO
WHO'S THIS?!
UP THERE ON THE CLIFF. HE SHOT THEM!!
NO...
...TATSUO?!

CALL. 17: TATSUO

VOL. 3

DRAGON

CONTENTS

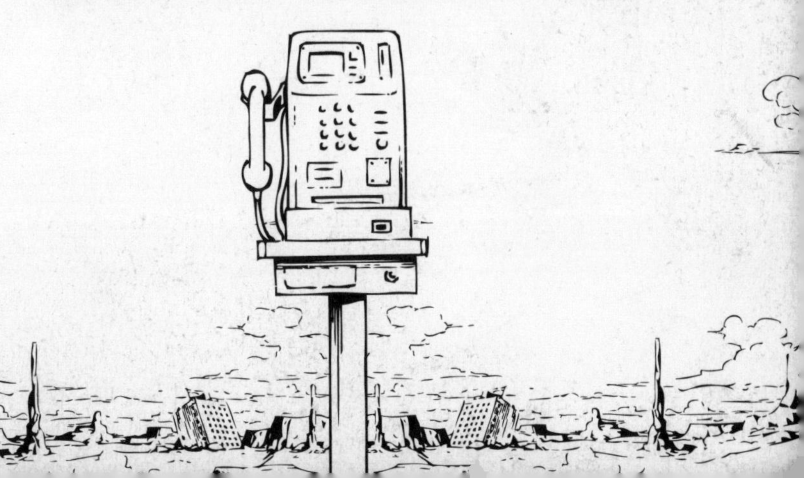

Characters

UNKNOWN

Story

AGEHA YOSHINA IS A STUDENT AT SHIRATAKI HIGH SCHOOL WHO HAPPENS UPON A RED TELEPHONE CARD EMBLAZONED WITH THE WORD PSYREN. SUSPECTING A LINK BETWEEN THE DISAPPEARANCE OF HIS CHILDHOOD FRIEND SAKURAKO AMAMIYA AND THE URBAN LEGEND OF THE PSYREN SECRET SOCIETY, AGEHA USES THE CARD AND FINDS HIMSELF CAUGHT UP IN A GAME OF LIFE-OR-DEATH IN THE PSYREN WORLD.

AGEHA SURVIVES AND RETURNS HOME TO MEET SAKURAKO'S MENTOR, MATSURI YAGUMO. HE LEARNS OF THE TERRIFYING RULES OF THE PSYREN GAME AND OF THE MENTAL POWER, PSI, THEIR ONLY HOPE OF SURVIVAL IN PSYREN WORLD. WHEN AGEHA AND HIS FRIENDS ARE SENT BACK TO PSYREN, THEY FIND THEMSELVES UNDER ATTACK BY A GIANT WORM AND A MEMBER OF THE BIZARRE TABOO TRIBE!

AGEHA YOSHINA

HIRYU ASAGA

SAKURAKO AMAMIYA

KABUTO KIRISAKI

OBORO MOCHIZUKI

SHONEN JUMP MANGA EDITION

PSYREN

3

DRAGON

Story and Art by
Toshiaki Iwashiro

PSYREN VOL. 3
SHONEN JUMP Manga Edition

STORY AND ART BY TOSHIAKI IWASHIRO

Translation/Camellia Nieh
Lettering/Annaliese Christman
Design/Sam Elzway, Matt Hinrichs
Editors/Joel Enos, Carrie Shepherd

Printed in the U.S.A.

Published by VIZ Media, LLC
P.O. Box 77010
San Francisco, CA 94107

10 9 8 7 6 5 4 3 2 1
First printing, March 2012

www.viz.com

PARENTAL ADVISORY
PSYREN is rated T for Teen and is recommended for ages 13 and up. This volume contains fantasy violence.
ratings.viz.com

www.shonenjump.com

Toshiaki Iwashiro

For the longest time, I haven't been able to get rid of the stiffness in my shoulders.

It's even making my head ache. Please, pain, go away!

Toshiaki Iwashiro was born December 11, 1977, in Tokyo and has the blood type of A. His debut manga was the popular *Mieru Hito*, which ran from 2005 to 2007 in Japan in *Weekly Shonen Jump*, where *Psyren* was also serialized.